FINAL IMPROVEMENT

REMEMBER YOUR PAST   **EVALUATE YOUR PRESENT**

PINPOINT YOUR FUTURE

A step by step strategy to ensure:
Your loved ones are genuinely empowered
Your house is in excellent order
Your life is truly honored

DAN MILLER, PASTOR

Xulon PRESS

FOR THOSE THAT I LOVE

———⟨∞⟩———

The information contained in this manual may be relatively <u>unimportant </u>to you until the moment that I leave this world. In the hours following that expected event, it will undoubtedly be the <u>most important </u>information available to you.

SIGNED _____

FINAL IMPROVEMENT

BY DAN MILLER
COPYRIGHT 2011
PRINTED IN THE UNITED STATES OF AMERICA

To Contact Dan Miller
P.O. Box 29071 Bellingham, WA 98228
Phone:360-510-3638   e-mail: <u>dan@millerz.info</u>

CONTENTS

———⊗⊗⊗———

INTRODUCTION

(Why this book is essential)

———⚬⚭⚬———

I truly hope that you will invest the time to thoughtfully enter the vital information on the following pages. During the past 35 years as a Pastor, I've had the privilege of serving people in very difficult situations. I've also worked for two funeral homes. These experiences have given me sober insight into what families face on the day that usually is the worst day of their life.

Most Pastors, Priest's, Rabbi's, Counselors, and others who give care to grieving people are very qualified, extremely thoughtful and do a great job helping people work through the grieving process. What we don't do well is prepare people for the "business side" of this somber occurrence. As a result, families are left vulnerable to one or more of the following scenarios.

<u>First</u>, I have been with many families on the day of a loved ones passing. Families expect this time to be reserved for grieving, hugs, tears and smiles. They want to share warm memories and receive much needed support from friends and family. Instead, after the initial and sometimes tragic first hours, families become overwhelmed with the requirements those hours present. Often they feel emotionally crushed, perplexed or angry and extremely stressed by the weight of decision making and fact gathering.

<u>Secondly</u>, it is not uncommon to see relational disintegration in families. Often, these are families that had been solid and caring people previous to the passing of their loved one. But something changed in the days following the death. I have seen loving family members become resentful and even hostile toward each other. Usually this was caused by personal claims and expectations on various items and assets owned by the deceased.

A <u>third</u> very common issue that I have sadly observed during this emotional and cloudy time, is that many families are desperately trying to say, "I love you" one more time.

They express this need by "emotionally overspending" on the funeral and cemetery choices. They incur unplanned and unnecessary debt, something the deceased surely would not have wanted.

It is never easy to think about or discuss our eventual death. Final Improvement is designed to help you with that. By using this book and planning ahead, you will be doing your family a significant service. This act of love will lessen their burdens and confusion in a multitude of ways. It will free them to focus on your life and their priorities. It will give you and your spouse (if married) an opportunity to plan together and it will help you to focus on the dignity, pride and value of your existence. Most importantly, you will not leave someone else with a burden that you could have lifted.

In this book you can record vital information that is necessary and immediately available to your loved ones. Often people who are grieving have a hard time processing and remembering these important facts and where to go to get the answers. You will guide your loved ones concerning your memorial wishes, provide them with the necessary historical information, your vital statistics and the location of important documents. You will be able to express your love and care ahead of time.

My desire is that when you pass on to the next life, you will leave your family in a secure place, empowered with knowledge, safe from hurtful division and equipped with the confidence they did what you would have wanted. They will be able to grieve their great loss in a meaningful and significant manner that will lead them to a positive healing process and wonderful memories of you.

Dan Miller

So teach us to number our days aright, that we may gain a heart of wisdom.
Psalms 90:12 NKJV

SECTION ONE

WHAT YOU WILL NEED
BUT DON'T WANT TO TALK ABOUT

IMMEDIATE CONTACTS

MY VITAL RECORDS AND MEDICAL HISTORY

MY FINANCIAL, LEGAL AND OTHER SIGNIFICANT INFORMATION

MY PERSONAL MEMORIAL INSTRUCTIONS

———⚬⚬⚬———

IMMEDIATE CONTACTS
TO NOTIFY
AT THE TIME OF MY PASSING

PRIMARY CONTACT PERSON:

Name_____Relationship_____Phone_____

FAMILY MEMBERS AND RELATIVES:

Name_____Relationship_____Phone_____
Name_____Relationship_____Phone_____
Name_____Relationship_____Phone_____
Name_____Relationship_____Phone_____
Name_____Relationship_____Phone_____
Name_____Relationship_____Phone_____
Name_____Relationship_____Phone_____
Name_____Relationship_____Phone_____
Name_____Relationship_____Phone_____

CLOSE FRIENDS:

Name_____Relationship_____Phone_____
Name_____Relationship_____Phone_____
Name_____Relationship_____Phone_____
Name_____Relationship_____Phone_____
Name_____Relationship_____Phone_____

ADVISORS:

Name_____Relationship_____Phone_____
Name_____Relationship_____Phone_____

ORGANIZATIONS TO BE NOTIFIED:

Church:_____Name_____Phone
Club:_____Name_____Phone
Lodge:_____Name_____Phone

OTHER KEY CONTACTS:

Funeral Home/Director:_____City_____Phone _____
Attorney: _____City_____Phone _____
Accountant:_____City_____Phone _____
Personal Physician _____City_____Phone _____
Clergy Person _____City_____Phone _____

The glory of friendship is not the outstretched hand, nor the kindly smile, nor the joy of companionship: it is the spiritual inspiration that comes to one when he discovers that someone else believes in him and is willing to trust him with his friendship. Ralph Waldo Emerson

Moments of kindness and reconciliation are worth having, even if the parting has to come sooner of later. Alice MunrO

MY VITAL RECORD

First Name	Middle	Last

Social Security Number	Date of Birth	Birthplace (City, County, State)

Current Address	City	State	Zip

Phone Number	Cell phone	E-mail Address

Marital Status (Circle One)   Single   Married   Widowed   Divorced

Race/Nationality

Spouse's Maiden Name	Marriage Date	Place	Date of Death

Father's Name   Deceased (check one) ☐ Y ☐ N

Mother's Maiden Name   Deceased (check one) ☐ Y ☐ N

Lifetime Occupation	Industry	Employer

Position Held/Job Title   No. of Years with Employer

Education Level Completed

High School	City	State	Yr. of Graduation

College/University	City	State	Yr. of Graduation

Degree(s) Certification(s) Received

"It was probably much happier to live in a small house,
and have Warwick Castle to be astonished at, than to live in
Warwick Castle and have nothing to be astonished at."
John Ruskin 1880's

MY MEDICAL HISTORY

This information could be vital to all of my immediate family and those of future generations. It has been known for years that certain diseases run in families. My medical history is a vital tool for helping you understand possible health risks. It can also be very important for doctors and researchers. It will enable them to be proactive in advising specific lifestyle changes to reduce those risks.

When reviewing my medical history, it is important to know which specific diseases to focus on. It can also be helpful to know, who in the family may have suffered certain diseases, their age when contracting the disease, if it was fatal, and their age at death.

Professionals, generally suggest that we collect at least three generations of medical history. Those most impacted a personal medical history are siblings, children, and parents. Also at risk may be grandchildren, nieces/nephews, aunts/uncles.

Below is a list of family members who have been diagnosed with the following diseases.

Diseases which are known to run in families include:
- Cardiovascular disease (including hypertension and stroke)
- Cancer
- Diabetes
- Mental Illness
- Circulatory Problems
- Osteoporosis
- Arthritis
- Obesity
- Seizures
- Alzheimer's or Dementia
- Other _____

Who		Disease	Age when Diagnosed	Age of Death (if related to this disease)
Dad	☐	_____	_____	_____
Mom	☐	_____	_____	_____

Me ☐ _____ _____ _____

Brother ☐ _____ _____ _____

Brother ☐ _____ _____ _____

Brother ☐ _____ _____ _____

Sister ☐ _____ _____ _____

Sister ☐ _____ _____ _____

Sister ☐ _____ _____ _____

Child ☐ _____ _____ _____

Child ☐ _____ _____ _____

Child ☐ _____ _____ _____

My allergies:

Drugs: 1._____ 2._____ 3._____

Food: 1._____ 2._____ 3._____

Pollen: 1._____ 2._____ 3._____

Insects: 1._____ 2._____ 3._____

My Doctor:_____ **Phone Number:**_____

My Specialist: _____ **Phone Number:**_____

I have a Living Will: ☐ Yes ☐ No
Location _____
Additional Comments: _____
_____
_____
_____

I am an Organ Donor: ☐ Yes ☐ No

Additional Comments Concerning About My Medical History:_____
_____
_____
_____
_____
_____
_____
_____
_____
_____
_____
_____
_____
_____
_____
_____
_____
_____
_____
_____
_____
_____
_____
_____

"It's not what happens to you that determine how far you will go in life; it is how you handle what happens to you". Zig Ziglar

"Life is 10 percent what you make it and 90 percent how you take it." Irving Berlin

FINANCIAL, LEGAL AND OTHER SIGNIFICANT INFORMATION

Federal and State agencies are holding in trust more then $400 billion in unclaimed assets until their legal owner comes forward. People open up savings and retirement accounts, acquire stocks and bonds or open safety deposit boxes. Many times they move away, die or have lifestyle changes and these assets are forgotten and unclaimed.

My Attorney: _____ phone_____

Location of Safety Deposit Box_____ Location of Key_____

I have a (revocable-irrevocable) trust. (yes) (no) Location _____
I have granted durable power of attorney to _____
I have an advance directive. (yes) (no). Location _____

Insurance

Life Insurance Benefits:

Location of Policies: _____

a. type: ☐ term (end date _____) ☐ whole life ☐ universal life ☐ group
   Ins. Co._____policy#_____Beneficiary(s)_____

b. type: ☐ term (end date_____) ☐ whole life ☐ universal life ☐ group
   Ins Co. _____policy# _____Beneficary (s)_____

c. type: ☐ term (end date_____) ☐ whole life ☐ universal life ☐ group
   Ins Co. _____policy#_____Beneficiary (s)_____

Life Insurance that I own on someone else:

Insured (s)_____ Policy Information_____
Insured (s)_ _____ Policy Information _____

Other Insurance:

Home owners Insurance: Company _____ **Phone#** _____
Policy Location_____**Policy #** _____

Disability Insurance: Company_____**Phone#**_____
Policy Location_____**Policy #** _____

Long Term Care Insurance: Company_____**Phone#**_____
Policy Location_____**Policy #** _____

Auto Insurance: Company_____ **Phone#**_____
Policy#_____**Death Benefit $** _____

Credit Card Insurance: Provider_____**Card #**_____
Phone#_____ **Death Benefit $**_____

Annuities

Annuity Contract: Company_____ **Phone#** _____
Policy # _____ **Contact Location** _____

Annuity Contract: Company _____**Phone#** _____
Policy # _____ **Contact Location** _____

Real Estate Holdings

Address: _____
Deed Location: _____
Description: _____

Address: _____
Deed Location: _____
Description: _____

Address: _____
Deed Location: _____
Description: _____

Address: _____
Deed Location: _____
Description: _____

Address: _____
Deed Location: _____
Description: _____

Banking

Bank _____ Branch_____ Phone#_____
Type ☐Checking #_____ ☐Savings #_____

Bank _____Branch _____Phone#_____
Type ☐Checking #_____ ☐Savings #_____

Bank _____Branch _____Phone#_____
Type ☐ Checking #_____ ☐ Savings #_____

*is there Life Insurance benefits with any of these accounts? _____

Credit Cards

☐ Visa   ☐ Master Card   ☐ Am. Express   ☐ Discover   ☐ Other
Account #_____ Exp. Date_____ Phone_____

☐ Visa   ☐ Master Card   ☐ Am. Express   ☐ Discover   ☐ Other
Account #_____ Exp. Date_____ Phone_____

☐ Visa   ☐ Master Card   ☐ Am. Express   ☐ Discover   ☐ Other
Account #_____ Exp. Date_____ Phone_____

☐ **Visa**   ☐ **Master Card**   ☐ **Am. Express**   ☐ **Discover**   ☐ **Other**
Account #_____ **Exp. Date**_____ **Phone**_____

☐ **Visa**   ☐ **Master Card**   ☐ **Am. Express**   ☐ **Discover**   ☐ **Other**
Account #_____ **Exp. Date**_____ **Phone**_____

Mutual Funds, Stocks, Bonds, C.D.'s

Location_____**Discription**_____**Value**_____
Location_____**Discription**_____**Value**_____
Location_____**Discription**_____**Value**_____
Location_____**Discription**_____**Value**_____

Vehicles and Other Assets

Type/Description _____**Location**_____

Type/Description _____**Location**_____

Type/Description _____**Location**_____

Type/Description _____**Location**_____

Type/Description _____**Location**_____

Type/Description _____**Location** _____

Liabilities

Lender _____ **Account #** _____ **Phone #**_____
   Purpose of Loan _____

Lender _____ **Account #** _____ **Phone #**_____
   Purpose of Loan _____

Lender _____ Account # _____ Phone #_____
    Purpose of Loan _____

Lender _____ Account # _____ Phone #_____
    Purpose of Loan _____

Computer Logins and Passwords

Account_____ Login_____ Password_____

Account_____ Login_____ Password_____

Account_____ Login_____ Password_____

Account_____ Login_____ Password_____

Rented Storage Units

Location of Unit_____
Unit Number_____ **Lock Combination or Key Location**_____

Location of Unit_____
Unit Number_____ **Lock Combination or Key Location**_____

Location of Unit_____
Unit Number_____ **Lock Combination or Key Location**_____

MY PERSONAL MEMORIAL INSTRUCTIONS

Soon after the arrangements are made, the service is over and the burial is complete, the haunting question that often remains in the mind of surviving spouse and family is: "did we do what our loved one would have wanted?"

By carefully filling out the following information, I want to provide peace and safety to you because you may be somewhat emotionally vulnerable during the next few days. Also, I want to eliminate intrusive and negative questioning from others that might want to second guess your decisions.

- ❖ Preferred Funeral Home/Mortuary/Crematorium _____
  City_____ Phone _____

- ❖ Name of Church/Hall/ Chapel where service will be held _____
  City _____ Phone_____

- ❖ Type of Service I Desire:
  - ☐ Complete Traditional Funeral Service (Burial or Cremation)
  - ☐ Graveside Entombment with Visitation proceeding
  - ☐ Simple Graveside (No Visitation)
  - ☐ None

  Note: Most Cemeteries charge extra for weekend Services

- ❖ Please Contact: ☐ Minister ☐ Priest ☐ Rabbi ☐ Bishop ☐Other _____
  To conduct my Service: Name_____ phone _____

- ❖ My Personal Preference for Burial:
  ☐ Vault ☐ Underground Vault ☐ Double Vault ☐ Mausoleum

  ☐ Ground Burial ☐ Cremation ☐ Green Burial

- ❖ If Cremation, what type of Disposition:
  ☐ Burial ☐ Niche ☐ Cremation Garden ☐ Scattered _____where

  ☐ Urn ☐ Other

- ❖ Type of Casket: ☐ Hardwood ☐ Metal ☐ Other

- ❖ Price Range I Desire: Modest _____ Medium _____ Maximum____

❖ Price Range of Vault (O.B. C) Modest ____ Medium____ Maximum____

❖ I own Burial Property at _____ Location of Deed_____

   Legal Description of Property_____ Crypt or Space #_____
   Lot #_____ Lawn Crypt or Mausoleum Space #_____

❖ I own: ☐ Memorial Marker ☐ Urn ☐ Vault (O.B.C) ☐ Flower Container ☐ Urn
   ☐Casket ☐ Opening and Closing Rights Paid For ☐_____other

❖ Memorial Plaque/Headstone Inscription_____
   Symbols or Emblems _____

❖ Additional Remarks/Special Instructions/Items to be placed with my remains

   _____
   _____

❖ Other Costs to Consider:
   • Removal and transfer of the deceased to Funeral Home
   • Care and preparation of the deceased
   • Embalming or Cremation
   • Use of Facility and Staff
   • Use of Limousine
   • Service at the Funeral Home
   • Flowers
   • Food for Reception
   • Physician, Nurse, Hospital, Medicine and Drugs
   • Minister, Musician (s)Fees
   • Preparing home for out of town guests. Food and Lodging

INSTRUCTIONS FOR MY SERVICE

❖ **CASKET:** ☐ Open During Service ☐ Closed During Service

❖ **Music Selections:**
Title of Music_____
Vocalists Name_____**Phone**_____
Organists/Pianists Name_____**Phone**_____

❖ **Special Readings:**

_____
Scripture/Poetry/Quotations　　　　　　**Readers Name/phone**

_____
Scripture/Poetry/Quotations　　　　　　**Readers Name/phone**

❖ **Floral Preference: Type and Color Preferred** _____

❖ **Flag:** ☐ Draped ☐ Folded ☐ Presented to _____

❖ **Clothing   Preference:**   _____
☐ Current Wardrobe ☐ New ☐ Other

❖ **Personal Accessories:**
☐ Wear Wedding Band ☐ Stays on or ☐ Return to _____
☐ Wear Eyeglasses ☐ Stays on or ☐ Return to _____
☐ Jewelry _____☐ Stays on or ☐ Return to_____
☐ Other Items _____

❖ **Participating Organizations (Fraternal/Military)**

_____
_____

❖ **Memorial Contribution Designation:**
_____**City**_____**State**_____
_____**City**_____**State**_____

❖ **Addition Information:** _____
_____
_____

❖ **Pallbearers' Names**   **Relationship**   **Phone #**

_____   _____   _____

_____   _____   _____

_____   _____   _____

_____   _____   _____

_____   _____   _____

_____   _____   _____

❖ **Honorary Pallbearers'**   **Relationship**   **Phone #**

_____   _____   _____

_____   _____   _____

_____   _____   _____

_____   _____   _____

_____   _____   _____

_____   _____   _____

❖ **Making Benefits Claims to Social Security**

Social Security Number: _____-_____-_____
Address of Nearest Social Security Office _____
Phone#_____

*Social Security may pay a lump sum death benefit to an eligible surviving widow, widower or eligible child to assist with final expenses. The actual amount payable is determined by past earnings. A three month processing period is not unusual before Social Security benefits actually begin. An application for lump sum death benefits must be made within two years after the death. The following documents may be necessary to make a claim for Social Security benefits:

- **Certified copies of the Death Certificate**
- **Certified copies of the Marriage License or Termination of the marriage decree**
- **Children's birth certificate**
- **Survivors Social Security Numbers**
- **Proof Widow/Widowers age is 62 or older**
- **W-2 or Schedule C earnings from the previous year**

Social Security Administration Toll Free Phone Number:
1-800-772-1213   www.ssa.gov

PERSONAL BEQUESTS

It is not uncommon for family members to experience hurt feelings because items of great value were divided in an unexpected manner. To avoid friction or division between family members or friends, I have listed below all family heirlooms and items of sentimental value.

ARTICLE   **BENEFICIARY**

_____   _____

_____   _____

_____   _____

_____   _____

_____   _____

_____   _____

_____   _____

_____   _____

_____   _____

_____   _____

_____   _____

_____   _____

_____   _____

_____   _____

_____   _____

_____   _____

_____   _____

_____   _____

_____   _____

_____   _____

_____   _____

_____   _____

_____   _____

Notes relating to the above decisions:

SECTION TWO

<u>THE STORY OF MY LIFE</u>

MEMORIES

MY FAMILY AND SOME PERSONAL WORDS

Memories

We do not remember days; we remember moments.
Cesare Pavese, the Burning Brand

Dear Family. On the following pages I have written about various events, relationships and milestones that helped define me and establish my personal destiny. These are the experiences that have brought to me both challenge and personal joy. My purpose is to share my history and hopefully to pass on something that may benefit you and future generations.

How I was raised (what life was like during my early years)

_____
_____
_____
_____
_____
_____
_____
_____
_____
_____
_____
_____
_____
_____
_____
_____
_____
_____
_____
_____
_____

And even if you were in some prison, the walls of which
let none of the sounds of the world come to your senses-
would you not then still have your childhood, that precious,
kingly possession, that treasure-house of memories?
Rainer Maria Rilke

Personal Challenges/Lessons Learned/Significant Triumphs in my life:

_____
_____
_____
_____
_____
_____
_____
_____
_____
_____
_____
_____
_____
_____
_____
_____
_____
_____
_____
_____
_____
_____
_____
_____
_____
_____
_____
_____
_____
_____
_____
_____
_____

Things that were hard to bear are sweet to remember - Seneca

Recollections of my Family:

_____
_____
_____
_____
_____
_____
_____
_____
_____
_____
_____
_____
_____
_____
_____
_____
_____
_____
_____
_____
_____
_____
_____
_____
_____
_____
_____
_____
_____
_____
_____
_____
_____
_____
_____
_____
_____
_____

Memory is a way of holding onto the things you love,
The things you are, the things you never want to lose.
From *The Wonder Years*

How my life was developed by what I did (jobs, career, other significant responsibilities):

_____
_____
_____
_____
_____
_____
_____
_____
_____
_____
_____
_____
_____
_____
_____
_____
_____
_____
_____
_____
_____
_____
_____
_____
_____
_____
_____
_____
_____
_____
_____
_____
_____
_____

The past is never dead, it is not even past.
William Faulkner

Major World Events, Technology and Other Changes During my Life Time

---

Everybody needs his memories. They keep the wolf of insignificance from the door
Saul Bellow

Other Important Memories and Personal Thoughts

_____

_____

_____

_____

_____

_____

_____

_____

_____

_____

_____

_____

_____

_____

_____

_____

_____

_____

_____

_____

_____

_____

_____

_____

_____

_____

_____

_____

_____

_____

_____

_____

_____

_____

_____

_____

_____

_____

MY FAMILY

INCLUDING PERSONAL WORDS TO EACH OF YOU

"The family is one of nature's masterpieces" George Santayana

NAME	ADDRESS	PHONE

Father
(address if living) _____

Mother
(address if living) _____

Spouse _____

"The happiest moments of my life have been the few which I have passed at home in the bosom of my family" Thomas Jefferson

Children:

_____
_____
_____
_____
_____
_____
_____
_____
_____
_____

"The family. We are a strange little band of characters trudging through life sharing diseases and toothpaste, coveting one another's desserts, hiding shampoo, borrowing money, locking each other out of rooms, inflicting pain and kissing to heal it in the same instant, loving, laughing, defending and trying to figure out the common thread that bound us all together." Erma Bombeck

Siblings:

_____
_____
_____
_____
_____
_____
_____
_____

Grandchildren and Great-Grandchildren:

_____
_____
_____
_____
_____
_____
_____
_____
_____
_____

Grandchildren and Great-Grandchildren continued:

_____
_____
_____
_____
_____
_____
_____
_____
_____

Those who have preceded me to the next life:

Name	Relationship	Date

"Family life is a bit like a runny peach pie – not perfect but who's complaining." P. Brault

PERSONAL WORDS TO MY FAMILY

TO MY SPOUSE
(ADDITIONAL PAGES AT BACK OF THIS BOOK)

_____

_____

_____

_____

_____

_____

_____

_____

_____

_____

_____

_____

_____

_____

_____

_____

_____

_____

_____

_____

_____

_____

_____

_____

_____

_____

_____

_____

_____

_____

TO EACH OF MY CHILDREN
(ADDITIONAL PAGES AT BACK OF THIS BOOK)

TO OTHER PEOPLE IN MY LIFE
(ADDITIONAL PAGES AT BACK OF THIS BOOK)

SECTION THREE

TOOL CHEST

WHAT TO DO AFTER THE FUNERAL

WHY A WILL IN NECESSARY

HOW TO FINANCE A FUNERAL

VETERAN'S BENEFITS

MEDICAID AND FINAL EXPENSE PROVISIONS

Glossary of terms

—⊱⊰—

AFTER THE FUNERAL
WHAT NEEDS TO BE DONE NEXT?

After the loss of a loved one, each one of us goes through a grieving process. During this time there may be a period of days, weeks or even longer when it is difficult to concentrate. Most people don't know what to do concerning the affairs of the deceased. However, there are very important legal and financial matters that require prompt attention. Following, is a list of items that need to be looked after. It may be important to ask for help from a friend or family member. Remember to check them off upon completion.

☐ *If your loved one was a veteran,* you may be able to get assistance with the funeral, burial plot and other benefits. The VA number is 1-800 827-1000. Look for other help in this manual in the Veterans section.

☐ *Obtain 10-15 copies of the Death Certificate* from your funeral director (you may need hard to get copies at a much later time).

☐ If your loved one was receiving Social Security benefits, *notify your local Social Security office* of the death, since these benefits will stop. The Social Security number is 1-800-772-1213. Overpayments will result in a difficult process of repayment. If you are a spouse, ask about your eligibility for increased benefits. Also, check on benefits that any minor children may be entitled to receive. Helpful pamphlets are available to you without cost. Ask for Social Security Survivor Benefits Publication numbers: 05-100-84 and 05-100-24

☐ *Contact the health insurance company or employer* regarding terminating coverage for the deceased while continuing coverage for others covered through the policy.

☐ *Contact the life insurance company* for all life policies. You will need to provide the policy number and a certified copy of the death certificate and fill out a claim form. If the deceased is named as the beneficiary on any other policy, arrange to have the name removed.

☐ If the deceased was working, *contact the employer for information* on pension plans, credit unions and union death benefits. *You will need a certified copy of the death certificate for each claim.*

☐ *Return credit cards of the deceased* with a certified copy of the death certificate, or notify the credit card company if you, as the survivor, want to retain use of the card.

☐ *Seek the advice of an accountant or tax advisor* about filing the deceased's tax return for the year of the death. Keep monthly bank statements on all individual and joint accounts that show the account balance on the day of death, since you will need this information for the estate tax return.

☐ *Arrange to change any joint bank accounts into your name.* If the deceased's estate is in trust, check with the Trust Department or Customer Service at the bank.

☐ *If the deceased owned a car,* transfer the automobile title into your name at the Secretary of State's Office, or if the estate is probated, through Probate Court.

☐ *Arrange to change stocks and bonds into your name.* Your bank or stockbroker will have the forms.

☐ *Make sure that important bills,* such as mortgage payments, continued to be paid.

HELPFUL RESOURCES:

- "The Mourning Handbook: The Most Comprehensive Resource Offering Both Practical and Compassionate Advice on Coping with All Aspects of Death and Dying" by Helen Fitzgerald

- "I Wasn't Ready to Say Goodbye: Surviving, Coping and Healing after the Sudden Death of a Loved One" by Brook Noel and Pamela Blair

- "How to Go On Living When Someone You Love Dies" by Therese Rando, Ph.D

- "What to Do When a Loved One Dies: a practical and compassionate guide to dealing with death on life's terms" by Eva Shaw (Dickens Press, 1994).

- "Step by Step: Your Guide to Making Practical Decisions When a Loved One Dies" by Ellen Shaw, (Quality Life Resources, 2001).

WHY A WILL IS NECESSARY

A will is a crucial document that transfers your property to designated persons at the time of your death. It is revocable, which means that it is subject to change until your death. If you die _intestate_, that is, without a will, you will lose your right to decide how your assets will be distributed and how your possessions will be divided. If minor children are left without parents, the Department of Social Services will be given guardianship. With a will, you (the "testator" if you are a man or "testatrix" if you are a woman) are in control of these matters. Though most people are aware of their need for a will, a Consumer Report article states that about 66% of us don't have one.

If you neglect this important task, it will leave your family in a compromised position. The assets and personal property that you intended for others, will be diluted and marginalized, by the legal expenses needed to secure them.

Many people have had a will drawn up but haven't looked at it in years. We move, someone passes away, a marriage dissolves or a new marriage begins. We have relational fallouts or someone is added to our family. Be sure to examine your will occasionally. Be certain that your intentions will be honored in the way you desire.

You should also name an "executor" (man) or "executrix" (woman). This trusted person will be charged with the fiduciary duty to carry out the terms and conditions of your will. Also, they will collect assets, pay debts and taxes and manage assets according to your intentions. The executor of a large estate will have a large task, but is usually rewarded by receiving a fee. Usually a percentage of the estate's value.

Probated assets will have to pass through a court if not included in your will. This may include real estate, cars, bank accounts, stocks and bonds, partnership interests, and other financial assets unless they are re-titled in a trust. A will does not cover non-probate assets, including insurance policies and annuities, qualified pension plans and property held in some trusts. However, if the estate is named as beneficiary of any asset, then the Will provisions will govern distribution.

John Denver left home one morning for a gratifying plane ride. He had no idea that he would never return. When he crashed into the bay and died, he left three children and no will. He had an estate worth about $20 million. Other famous people who died without a will include; Howard Hughes, Martin Luther King, Jr., Sonny Bono, Cass Elliot (Mamas & the Papas), Buddy Holly and Tiny Tim. Presidents Abe Lincoln, Andrew Johnson, Ulysses S. Grant and James Garfield, also did not leave a will. These people are just a few examples of those who pass on leaving their estates vulnerable to out-side influences.

The shortest known legal will in history is that of Bimia Rishi of Delhi, India.
His will dated February 9, 1995, translated from Hindi is "all to son".

Information About
My Will

My Will was prepared by my attorney, _____(name), on_____(date).

The location of his/her office is_____(Address) _____(City) _____ (State).

His/her Phone Number is: _____.

The location of my Will is _____.

My Executor/Executrix is:

_____Name
_____Address
_____(City)_____State _____(Zip)
_____(Phone)

To live in the hearts we leave behind is not to die.
Thomas Campbell, Hollowed Ground

YOUR FINAL EXPENSE

"The average funeral in the U.S is now over $6,500. That doesn't include cemetery costs like opening and closing fees, a plot and a memorial marker, which can easily increase the expense to well over $10,000".* Funeral costs vary greatly depending upon the individual funeral home and the city in which they are located. They can range from less than $1,000 for a simple cremation in one city, to well over $500,000 for a service and burial in a private family crypt, in a city a short driving distance away. Regardless of the cost and the fact that at some time arrangements will need to be made for all of us, a full "79 percent of seniors report that they have not done any comparison shopping or made any arrangements". * Below are some common strategies that are used in our culture to cover the expense of dying.

LIFE INSURANCE OR OTHER ASSETS

Many couples plan to use a Life Insurance policy or their savings to pay for their funeral expenses. A financial challenge may come at a later date if one or both of them suffers a seriously illness, handicap, or incapacitation. It is not uncommon for a large portion of the assets to be needed for the unplanned expenses of later years. Besides health care, there are other costs like, durable medical equipment, in home care and home remodel for safety and mobility issues. The reality is that dying is expensive and sometimes starts years before the final breath is taken.

THE PRE-PAID FUNERAL HOME POLICY

"Among the 20 million individuals who have prepaid for funerals or burials, 53 percent paid the entire cost as a lump sum, while an additional 44 percent are paying in installments over time".* It could be a smart strategy to go to a local funeral home and make arrangements for funeral expenses. A well established funeral home will have a large number of people who have "pre-purchased" a funeral plan.

A funeral plan may work fine for many people but there could be a downside. Before investing in an expensive funeral plan you should consider the following:

❖ You may decide to move to another area of the country to be with the kids, because of the economy or you like a warmer climate. You may not want to be buried where you live now.

❖ Do you ever leave the state or the country? If you are far away on vacation and die, some plans will only pay allow for the shipment of cremated remains and a burial plan would be wasted.

❖ Many funeral homes have changed hands during the past two decades. And at times the results have been less than stellar for those with contracts. The new owners may not honor important details in existing contracts. It could be too late when you find out.

❖ Unfortunately, funeral homes and cemeteries do go bankrupt at times. It doesn't happen often, but when it does it creates major problems for the property owners. It's devastating when elderly people find out that the funeral plan they purchased decades before was lost in a cemetery bankruptcy. They are fortunate if they retain their plots. Often other goods and services that were purchased earlier were forfeited in the bankruptcy and present day prices are much higher.

❖ A couple buys a combined plan, expecting to be buried together. Years later either through death or divorce, there is a new partner. The previous burial arrangements may not be desirable.

THE MASS MAILER

Seniors are inundated with mailings from big National companies with "to good to be true offers". These policies have value but some could be very expensive in the years ahead. It is important to note what is *not* stated clearly. READ THE FINE PRINT! The positive aspect of these policies is that they have a very low premium (to start with) and if you were to die in a few years, they would serve their purpose. The problem is most people will outlive the first few years. A careful reading of the small print may reveal a few undesirable aspects. Consider a few of these offers.

1. One offer states, "the above low rate is for the first 5 years. Rates change after the 5th and 10th years at which time the policy becomes a whole life policy...In the first 10 years rates cannot change because of your health". You might ask, what's wrong with that? Notice two phrases: (a)the rate changes in years 5 and 10. There is no mention what that rate will be. After the 10th year, it becomes a whole life policy. The rate change could be substantial and you may not be able to afford it later in life. (b)After the10th year, if your health has deteriorated, watch out. The rates have gone up two

times already, and it becomes a whole life policy with rates based on your health at that time.

2. The second mail order policy proudly states, "just $43.50 a month for $10,000. Rates will not change with age. No medical examine. You can keep the policy as long as you live. Rates will not change with age". It sounds like you will always pay the same premium. But, <u>rates are based on five year age bands</u>. So the rates for the initial age band will not change. However, in 5 years you will be in the predetermined second age band. Your premium will be higher based on the age band of the initial plan. Every five years after, you can expect an increase in rates according to the age band.

3. This cagey advertisement gets a lot of results for the insurance company and is a great deal for the purchaser, if they die right away. The first month is only $1.00. Along with having very high long term premiums, "at age 80 your policy terminates". Eighty is not old anymore. You've paid your premiums for years, but the day after your 80th birthday, it's gone. No coverage when you need it the most. Sorry, the kids will have to pay for your funeral expenses. You will be much better off compare insurance policies from local companies that specialize in final expense insurance plans.

FINAL EXPENSE INSURANCE

Rather than using your regular the life insurance policy for burial expenses, another option is to purchase a separate Final Expense policy or Burial Policy. These policies pay quickly, are relatively inexpensive, and offer policy amounts from $1000 to $50,000. The proceeds can go to any chosen beneficiary or even a non-profit organization

There are many excellent "funeral" or "final expense" policies available through highly rated Life Insurance Companies or at some funeral homes. It is important to look for significant elements in a policy to determine the best value and most complete provisions. Once purchased the owner should be covered anywhere in the world for the policy amount. These policies are usually Whole Life Policies. The benefits will be available to the beneficiary regardless of the owner's age or physical condition at time of death. Below are some key features of these policies.

- ❖ Issue ages to age 85.
- ❖ Policy continues for life and is none cancellable as long as premiums are paid.
- ❖ No medical exam or blood work required, only a simple health questionnaire.

❖ Benefits paid directly to the beneficiary or non-profit organization of your choice. Many people will purchase a separate policy specifically to leave a gift for their <u>church, charity or other non-profit organization</u>.
❖ Benefits remain level regardless of your age at the time of death.

❖ Rates remain level and will never increase.
❖ Polices have a defined pay off period.
❖ Benefits are not subject to federal income tax.
❖ Policy value increases to keep pace with inflation.

• Statistics from the National Funeral Directors Association. Averages for this State are consistent with the National Average. Funeral /Burial costs double every 10 to 12 years.

COMMON FUNERAL EXPENSES

Funeral:

- o Professional Funeral Staff Service Fees
- o Pick up and Preparation of the body
- o Transportation To or From Another Funeral Home
- o Embalming (if necessary)
- o Cremation Process (for cremation only)
- o Use of Staff and facilities
- o Casket or Urn
- o Outer Burial Container
- o Visitation and Viewing
- o Funeral or Memorial Service
- o Graveside Service
- o Hearse
- o Limo Service for Family Members
- o Acknowledgement Cards
- o Obituary Notices
- o Death Certificates (recommended min. 10)
- o Clergy and Musician Honorariums
- o Flowers
- o Burial Garments and Accessories
- o Gifts or Donations (Pallbearers, Church, etc.)

Cemetery:

- o Grave Space, Crypt, Columbarium or Niche Wall
- o Opening and Closing of Grave
- o "Green" Burial Option
- o Grave Outer Burial Container or Liner
- o Perpetual Care of Grave Site
- o Grave/Crypt/Mausoleum Marker or Monument

Other Expenses:

- o Travel Costs for Family/Friends
- o Reception (Hall or Church rental, food, drinks, etc.)
- o Legal Expenses
- o State Sales Tax

VETERAN'S BENEFITS

The nearest Veteran's Administration office is located in _____ (City).

Veteran's, who at the time of death were,

- entitled to a pension or compensation
- died while hospitalized or living in a VA facility or other facility at VA expense
- were discharged or retired from service due to a disability incurred or aggravated in the line of duty, or
- are indigent with no claim for their remains, may be entitled to payments for a burial plot at a VA cemetery, a funeral, burial, flag and/or a grave marker or headstone supplied by the VA.

Important military records

Branch of Military_____ Rank_____
Service Serial Number_____ DD214(location)_____
Enlistment Date_____ Discharge Date_____
Certified Copy of Death Certificate
War or Conflicts Served in_____
Medals/Honors/Citations_____

Veteran's administration toll free phone number:
1-800-827-1000

GOT YOUR BACK

I am a small and precious child, my dad's been sent to fight.
The only place I'll see his face is in my dreams at night.
He will be gone too many days for my young mind to keep track.
I may be sad, but I'm proud. My daddy's got your back.

I am a caring mother, my son has gone to war.
My mind is filled with worries that I have never known before.
Every day I try to keep my thoughts from turning black.
I may be scared, but I am proud. My son has got your back.

I am a strong loving wife, with a husband soon to go.
There are time I'm terrified in a way most never know.
I bite my lip, and force a smile as I watch my husband pack.
I may be scared, but I am proud. My husband's got your back.

I am a Soldier, serving proudly...standing tall.
I fight for freedom, yours and mine, by answering this call.
I do my job while knowing, the thanks it sometimes lacks.
Say a prayer that I'll come home'
IT'S ME WHO'S GOT YOUR BACK!!
By: Autumn Parker

MY MILITARY STORY

My military story continued

MEDICAID AND FINAL EXPENSE PROVISIONS

Many older people are very concerned about paying for care during the last chapter of their lives. Life expectancies are increasing, the economy is challenging the strength of any acquired assets and the price of care is skyrocketing. As a result, a high percentage of people living in care facilities rely on Medicaid to pay for their care.

Medicaid provides medical treatment, including nursing home care for low income individuals who are over 65, blind or disabled. This program is funded by federal and state governments jointly.

Unlike Social Security, Medicaid is based on an individuals need and each person may need to take certain measures to become eligible. To be eligible a person must have assets that are very limited. A person may be required to "spend down" his or her assets to qualify. It is only when a person's assets reach this predetermined level, Medicaid will provide funding for qualified care facilities.

There are several methods to "spend down" assets to reach these specified limits. One way is to prepay funeral expenses, either by a lump sum payment or by reducing monthly income by using a final expense funeral plan. This concept has the following advantages:
1) The policy amount and premium can be adjusted to a level that will satisfy "spend down" requirements.
2) Funeral arrangements are a necessary expense that will need to be covered eventually. This proactive approach will take the burden off the shoulders of the survivors.
3) By using the pre payment plan for final expense coverage, the beneficiary(s) of the plan may receive tax free benefits from the unused proceeds of the policy.

The requirements for qualifying for Medicaid eligibility include the following:
> Be a U.S citizen living in the United States
> Be over 65, disabled or blind
> Have a "medical necessity" requiring skilled nursing care
> Medical and nursing home expenses exceed income
> Meet the income cap. The applicant cannot make more than approximately $2000 a month in most states.

➢ Have limited assets (usually less than $2,000, excluding a home). Special rules may also cover and applicant's assets and how they were used up to five years before an application to Medicaid is made. Other benefits and exclusions may apply to a spouse not living in a care facility. It is very important to see an Elder Law Attorney for specific advice.

Examples of assets are as follows:
   ➢ Checking/Savings Accounts
   ➢ Mutual Funds
   ➢ Stocks/Bonds
   ➢ Deferred Annuities
   ➢ Cash value of most life insurance policies
   ➢ Revocable living trusts
   ➢ 401K/IRA/Keoghs
   ➢ Burial Trusts beyond a minimum amount

GLOSSARY OF TERMS

A

After Care – Services available to families after the death of a loved one. Provided by funeral homes, churches and other non-profit groups to give support and furnish educational materials and resources.

Anatomical Donation – Donating the organs or tissue of a deceased person to another person to improve their health or save their life.

Arrangement Room – A separate room in the funeral home that is used to make the necessary arrangements with the family of the deceased.

Autopsy – an inspection of the body after death by a medical doctor in order to determine the cause of death. Not always required.

B

Basic Services – Services provided by the funeral home staff including: transporting the deceased, coordinating funeral details, assisting with administration tasks such as completing a death certificate, applying for benefits, etc.

Bereaved – The immediate family of the deceased. One who is suffering from grief upon the death of a loved one.

Body Donation – Donating the entire body for the purposes of medical science, research and education. If the medical facility already has the required number of donations at the time of death, the body may be refused by the organization and the family would need to proceed with normal funeral arrangements.

Burial – (Internment). The placing of the body in an underground chamber.

Burial Certificate or Permit. A legal document issued by the local government authorizing burial. The permit may authorize earth burial or cremation.

Burial Garments – Wearing apparel made especially for the deceased.

Burial Vault (Outer Burial Container) – A concrete, wood or metal structure that the casket is placed in. It is required by most cemeteries. The purpose is to keep the grave from collapsing after burial.

C

Casket – A container made of wood, metal or plastic into which the deceased is placed for burial. Sometimes referred to as a "coffin". A casket can be purchased at a funeral home, a store such as Costco or built at home.

Casketing – A term used by funeral professionals. It is the placing of the body in the casket upon the competition of embalming, dressing and cosmetizing.

Celebration of Life – An opportunity for friends and family to reflect on the life of the deceased rather than the death. Usually anecdotes are shared by those present. These stories focus on the positive memories and contributions of the deceased.

Certified Death Certificate – A legalized copy of the original certificate, issued upon request by the local government for the purpose of substantiating various claims by the family of the deceased such as insurance and other death benefits.

Chapel – a large room of the funeral home in which the funeral service is held.

Closed Casket – describes a visitation or ceremony in which the body is in a closed casket, not available for viewing.

Columbarium – A granite wall that is used to house cremated remains.

Committal Service – The final portion of the funeral service. At the gravesite the last words are said before the deceased is interred or entombed.

Coroner – A public official whose duty it is to investigate the cause of death if it appears to be from other than natural causes, or if there was no physician in attendance for a long time prior to death.

Cosmetology – The use of cosmetics to restore life like appearance to the deceased.

Cremated Remains – The remaining elements of the human body after the cremation process is complete, sometimes referred to as cremains.

Cremation – The process of using concentrated heat to reduce the human remains to ashes. Prior body weight is reduced by ninety five percent.

Cremation Casket – A special combustible casket that is used specifically for cremation. This casket can be used for viewing the body prior to cremation.

Cremation Permit - A certificate issued by local government authorizing cremation of the deceased.

Crematory or Crematorium – A distinct room in the mortuary or in a remote facility, a place where the cremation process is preformed.

Crypt – An underground chamber or a wall vault in a mausoleum, used to permanently hold human remains.

D

Death Certificate – A legal paper signed by the attending physician showing the legal cause of death and other vital statistical data pertaining to the deceased. Certified copies of the death certificate are required to file various claims such as insurance or death benefit claims. These additional certificates can be ordered through the funeral director.

Death Benefits – When a loved one dies, survivors may be eligible for benefits from Social Security or the Veteran's Administration.

Direct Burial – A burial with no viewing or visitation, usually consisting of care, transportation and the burial of the remains. A small ceremony may be held at the graveside in some situations.

Direct Cremation – The cremation occurs without a previous ceremony, viewing or visitation.

Dirge – A song or hymn of grief or lamentation, used to accompany funeral rites.

Display Room – The room in a funeral home in which caskets, urns, burial garments, memorial markers and vaults are displayed.

Disposition – The final resting place for the body or for the cremated remains. Choices include the burial of the body in the earth or a mausoleum; burial, scattering or deposit of cremated remains in an urn for placement in a niche or taking home; donation of the body to a research facility; or burial at sea.

E

Embalming – A process after death occurs in which the body is chemically treated by injection of an antiseptic through the veins and arteries for temporary preservation. This procedure includes disinfecting, preserving and restoring the human remains to natural life-like appearance. This preservation is intended to allow for adequate time to plan for a funeral service.

Entombment – The placing of human remains in a crypt or mausoleum.

Epitaph – An inscription on a tomb or grave in memory of the one buried there. A brief statement commemorating a deceased person.

Estate – The assets, liabilities and net worth left by a person at death.

Estate Tax – A tax in the form of a percentage of the taxable estate that is imposed on a property owner's right to transfer the property to others after his or her death.

Eulogy – A brief speech that offers praise and celebrates the life of the person who has died.

F

Family Car – The limousine in the funeral procession set aside for the privacy of close friends and family members.

Final Rites – The funeral service.

Funeral Arrangements – The funeral director's conference with the family for the purpose of completing financial and service details of a funeral.

Funeral Director – A mortician or undertaker, licensed by the State to conduct the funeral process including the legal arrangements, serving the family and overseeing the funeral service.

Funeral Escort – Individuals who escort a funeral procession, such as law enforcement officers.

Funeral Home – (Mortuary) A building used for the purpose of embalming, arranging and conducting funerals. The word funeral home came about in years ago when people held funerals and prepared bodies in their homes.

Funeral Procession – Two or more vehicles accompanying the remains of a deceased person, usually transporting remains to a final resting place.

Funeral Service – The religious service or other committal rites conducted immediately before final disposition of the body.

Funeral Spray – A collective mass of cut flowers sent to the home of the deceased or to the funeral home as a floral tribute to the deceased.

G

General Price List – A list of prices detailing services rendered by a funeral home. The Federal Trade Commission requires this list to be made available to anyone who requests it.

Graveside Service – A funeral ceremony held at the graveside.

Grave Liner – Also called an *outer burial container.* A receptacle made of concrete, metal or wood into which the casket is placed as an extra precaution in protecting the remains from the elements. This is required in most cemeteries to prevent the collapse of a grave after burial.

Green Funeral – Describes a funeral, cremation and burial options that are eco-friendly. The casket is made of biodegradable material and chemicals are not used in the preparation of the body for burial.

Grieving – A natural process that includes experiencing deep sadness after the loss of a loved one.

H

Head Stone – A granite or marble monument or a bronze plaque used to identify specific graves in the cemetery

Hearse (Funeral Coach)– A vehicle designed and used for transporting the deceased.

Honorary Pallbearers – Friends or members of a religious, social or fraternal organization who act as an escort or honor guard for the deceased. Honorary pallbearers do not carry the casket.

Hospice – An organization, staffed mainly by volunteers, dedicated to the care of the terminally ill who choose to die at home.

I

Immediate Burial – The direct disposition of the deceased without a formal viewing, visitation or ceremony.

Inquest – An official inquiry or examination usually before a jury to determine the cause of death.

In State – The custom of availing the deceased for viewing by relatives and friends prior to or after the funeral service.

Interment – The act of burial

Internment Right – The legal permission to inter the remains of the deceased in a specific place, within the cemetery

Inurnment – When the urn containing the ashes of the deceased are placed in a cemetery niche.

L

Last Testament – A will.

Lawn Crypt – A pre-built underground chamber used to bury human remains.

Lead Car – The vehicle in which the funeral director and sometimes the clergyman rides. When the procession is formed, the lead car moves to the head of it and leads the procession to the church and/or cemetery.

Limousine – An automobile designed to seat five or more persons behind the driver's seat. It is used to transport family members from the residence to the funeral home, church, cemetery or any other facility for a funeral or memorial ceremony.

M

Mass Cards – A card indicating that a Mass for the deceased has been arranged.

Mausoleum – A building especially designed to hold human remains above ground rather than being buried underground.

Medical Examiner – An official person who examines a body after death to determine the cause of death

Memorial – A granite, marble or brass grave marker in the cemetery used to identify the final resting place of the deceased.

Memorial Donation – A memorial contribution specified to a particular cause or charity, usually in lieu of flowers.

Memorial Service - A ceremony held in honor of the deceased. The body is not present at this service.

Military Funeral Honors – A service provided by law to honor the life of an eligible veteran if requested by the family of the veteran. The service includes, a military honor guard consisting of a minimum of two military services personal. The guard will fold and present an American flag to the family as well as play taps on a bugle or electronically.

Monument – A granite (at times marble) stone, used in a cemetery to identify the final resting place of a person. The family name and the individual names of those buried in the plot along with their dates of birth, death and other information depending on the wishes of the family.

Mourner – One who is present at the funeral out of affection or respect for the deceased

Motorcycle Escort – An escort arranged at the request of the funeral director to guide the funeral procession from the funeral service to the place of burial.

N

Next of Kin – The nearest living relative of the deceased.

Niche – A space designated in a special cemetery wall or in a mausoleum to hold an urn containing a persons cremated remains.

O

Obituary – A notice of a person's death placed in the local newspaper and often used in a funeral or memorial service.

Open Casket – A casket that is left open for the viewing of the deceased. Some times due to the circumstances surrounding the death or because of the wishes of the deceased or the family, the casket is left closed.

Opening and Closing of the Grave – The process provided by cemetery personal that includes proper boundary location, the digging of the grave and the backfilling after the placement of the remains.

Organ Donation – The honorable, pre-planned choice of the deceased or the immediate decision of the family of the deceased to donate certain vital organs or tissue for the purpose of transplanting them into another person

Outer Burial Container – Same as burial vault.

Ossuary – A depository for the bones of the dead.

P

Pall – A religious cloth that is draped over a coffin during the funeral service.

Pall Bearers – People who carry the casket as needed during the funeral service.

Plot – A cemetery space used for the burial of human remains.

Pre-Need, Pre-Planning or Pre-Arranging – The process of putting in place all of the necessary elements of ones funeral services before death occurs. It includes funding arrangements, specific funeral requests and the purchase of some or all of the necessary goods and services for ones funeral.

Procession – The vehicular movement of the funeral from the place where the funeral service was conducted to the cemetery. May also apply to a church funeral where the mourners follow the casket as it is brought into and taken out of the church

R

Register – A book made available by the funeral director for recording the names of people visiting the funeral home to pay their respects to the deceased. Also has space for entering other data such as name, dates of birth and death of the deceased, name of the officiating clergyman, place of interment, time and date of service, list of floral tributes, etc.

Reposing Room – A room of the funeral home where a body lies in state from the time it is casketed until the time of the funeral service.

Retort – The name for the machine that is used to cremate the body.

S

Scattering – The act of depositing the cremated remains in a cemetery garden, at sea, in the forest or in another place that was meaningful to the deceased.

Sea Burial – Typically used for one who has died at sea or Navy personnel. Sea burials must be authorized, be a in a minimum of 600 feet of water and be a least three miles from land.

Slumber Room or a State Room – A room equipped with usual furniture and a bed upon which the deceased is placed prior to casketing. The body, appropriately dressed, lies in state on the bed.

Social Security Death Benefit – A one time payment payable to the surviving spouse if alive or to a child who was eligible for benefits in the month of recorded death. Currently the benefit is $255. Typically the funeral home where services are provided will process the paperwork for this benefit. For up to date information call 1-800 772-12113.

Spiritual Banquet – A Roman Catholic practice involving specific prayers, such as Masses and Rosaries offered by an individual or a group for a definite purpose

Survivor – The persons outliving the deceased, particularly the immediate family.

T

Taps – A bugle call or electronic recording played at military funerals.

Traditional Service – A religious service with the body present usually preceded by visitation.

Tribute – An acknowledgement of gratitude, respect, or admiration of the deceased. Evidence attesting to some praiseworthy quality or characteristic.

U

Undertaker – Same as a funeral director.

Urn – A container into which cremated remains are placed, or in which they are kept. May be made of various materials, including wood, marble or metal.

Urn Vault – A small reinforced container used for housing an urn in the ground. The Urn Vault acts the same as a burial vault does for a casket – to help protect the surrounding ground from collapsing.

V

VA Death Benefits – A burial allowance is available from the Veterans Benefits Administration to eligible veterans. It includes free cemetery property in a national cemetery (there are 131 national cemeteries), the opening and closing of the grave, perpetual care, a government headstone or marker, a burial flag and a Presidential memorial certificate provided at no cost to the family. In a private cemetery the burial benefits at a minimum include a government headstone or marker, a burial flag and a presidential memorial certificate. For information call 1-800-827-1000. See VA form #40-1130

VA Markers – The VA furnishes upon request, at no charge to the applicant, a standard Government headstone or marker for the grave of any deceased eligible veteran in any cemetery around the world. If the Veteran chooses cremation an engraved niche cover (shutter) will be provided.

Vault – A burial chamber underground or partly so. Also includes I meaning the outside metal or concrete container.

Video Tribute – a memorial DVD that uses photographs relating to the life of the deceased.

Vigil – A Roman Catholic religious held on the eve of the funeral service.

Visitation – A period of time set aside for friends and family to visit the family of the person who has died.

W

Wake – A watch over the deceased, sometimes lasting the entire night preceding the funeral.

Glossary information provided by various sources including: Bliley Funeral homes of Virginia, Lynn-Stone Funeral Home and the Ontario Funeral Service Association.

TO MY SPOUSE
-CONTINUED

_____

_____

_____

_____

_____

_____

_____

_____

_____

_____

_____

_____

_____

_____

_____

_____

_____

_____

_____

_____

_____

_____

_____

_____

_____

_____

_____

_____

_____

_____

_____

_____

_____

_____

_____

_____

_____

_____

TO EACH OF MY CHILDREN
-CONTINUED

TO OTHER SIGNIFICANT PEOPLE IN MY LIFE
-CONTINUED

CPSIA information can be obtained at www.ICGtesting.com
Printed in the USA
BVOW051339310112

281842BV00002B/1/P